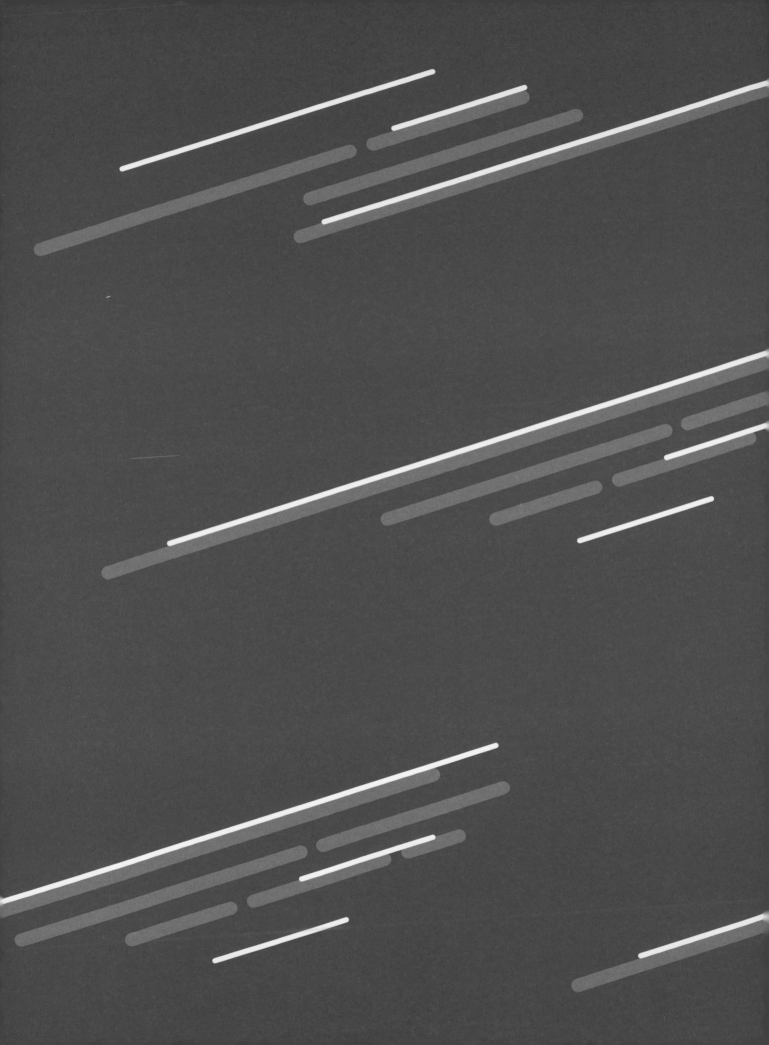

THE DAD ANNUAL

Michael Spicer

summersdale

THE DAD ANNUAL

An Hachette UK Company
www.hachette.co.uk

Summersdale Publishers Ltd
Part of Octopus Publishing Group Limited
Carmelite House
50 Victoria Embankment
LONDON
EC4Y 0DZ
UK

www.summersdale.com

Printed and bound in Poland

ISBN: 978-1-78783-298-5

Substantial discounts on bulk quantities of Summersdale books are available to corporations, professional associations and other organizations. For details contact general enquiries: telephone: +44 (0) 1243 771107 or email: enquiries@summersdale.com.

CONTENTS

What Type of Dad Are You?

CHECK THE "DAD TYPE" THAT YOU MOST RELATE TO FROM THE LIST BELOW.

BRAINY DAD

Knowledgeable without being interesting. You will always deconstruct jokes told to you. You will regularly state that you don't watch TV even though you have four.

SPORTY DAD

You're very competitive. You will make your children support your team because it's important boys and girls understand the feeling of disappointment from a very early age. You always ensure fair play. You always have the tidiest scorecard after a game of crazy golf.

LOW-MAINTENANCE PLAYTIME DAD

Your favourite game with your youngest is when they ride your leg like a horse because that means you can stay sitting on the sofa eating snacks. You're purposely bad at seeking during hide-and-seek. In fact, you spend the first half hour not seeking at all. For any kind of shooting game, you always ensure you're a baddie who gets shot first so you can have a quick nap while you're on the floor.

CREATIVE DAD

You love a craft shop. You see a huge sheet of coloured paper and immediately get ten ideas. You start the weekend building a cardboard rocket "for fun" and by Sunday night you're a NASA scientist barring your children from going anywhere near it. You make costumes and props for your children and then can't actually play with them because you need two days off with nervous exhaustion.

NERD DAD

Dedicated gamer. Sci-fi enthusiast. You will gladly play with your children's Star Wars figures – with or without your children. You get annoyed if you see your child playing with characters from both the Marvel Universe and the DC Universe.

CAUTIOUS DAD

PAW Patrol is banned because it's not a sensible business model. You can't take your child to the playground without a risk assessment. Every friend is vetted before a play date. You'll go along with the idea of Santa Claus but when it comes to the Tooth Fairy, you have to draw the line.

DIY DAD

You believe yourself to be better than all tradespeople because you once installed a tap without flooding your neighbourhood. Meticulous. Measured. You always put tools back in their designated grooves in the toolbox (or make sure it's all down flat so you can at least close it again).

CHEF DAD

You wear oven gloves over your shoulder like a fashion accessory. Your kitchen is your domain. You say "make room, make room, make room" when you take anything out of the oven. You thought everything you cooked was a disaster – until you discovered the word "rustic".

OUTDOOR DAD

You will always opt for clothes that suit your environment rather than, you know, nice clothes. You're in tune with nature, even if nature doesn't care much for you. You can put a tent up in 15 minutes – on the eighth attempt. Sometimes you'll even leave your phone at home because it's so liberating to be accompanied by nothing but birdsong, fresh air and an iPad.

CAR DAD

Drinking, eating and talking about drinking and eating are banned from your car. You're such an expert at weaving the seatbelt through a child's car seat that you've considered putting it on your résumé. You don't like the idea of a driverless car but you would like to own one even if just to put your dog in it wearing a chauffeur's hat.

ANAGRAMS

The following anagrams relate to your dream of becoming a musician. Good luck! (With the anagrams, not your career as a musician.)

WORDS:

1. RIDING MOPS BAN (9, 4)

2. DR C NASTI'S FIERCE E-FIT (8, 11)

3. GOOGLIN' SO (5, 4)

4. MALL ROUTS (5, 4)

5. SICKO TROPE TALES (4, 6, 5)

6. BASSER JOEL RIPPON (6, 3, 2, 5)

7. BEE BONKED WHY (7, 5)

ANSWERS:

1. PROMISING BAND 2. ARTISTIC DIFFERENCES 3. GOING SOLO 4. SMALL TOUR 5. POOR TICKET SALES 6. PROPER JOB IN SALES 7. WEEKEND HOBBY

TOP 10

MEN'S TOILETRIES

1 Soothing shaving gel: soothing gels have replaced old-fashioned harsh foams for good. The days of looking like you're eating a huge marshmallow are over.

2 Invigorating body wash: for those mornings when you need a shower to give you purpose in life because your brain's fed up with doing the job.

3 Muscle reviving gel: for those of you who have muscles, or who at least have an idea of where they used to be.

4 Rejuvenating moisturizer with organic sweet almond oil, jojoba, sunflower seed oil, bergamot and grapefruit: it's not a fancy moisturizer if it doesn't also make you hungry.

5 Anti-fatigue eye serum: for those men who work hard and play hard (and binge-watch *RuPaul's Drag Race* on Netflix).

6 Massage oils: perfect for soothing muscles that have perhaps tensed up with worry over how much you spend every week on massage oils.

7 Old-style shaving kit: for those times when you want a traditional barbershop shave but don't want to feel like you could be on the end of a clean Mafia hit at any moment.

8 Beard roller: for those with unwieldy face fuzz. We're not sure what it does, but if you own one, you'll feel like a hipster rather than, say, a 39-year-old man with a mortgage who doesn't know anything about subculture but does know all the words to the *Top Wing* theme thanks to having three children under seven.

9 Beard moisturizer: once you've rolled your beard – whatever that means – it makes sense to moisturize your beard too – whatever that means. There are plenty of beard moisturizers out there to condition and soften the hair so you look less like an unkempt shrub and more like a... well-kempt shrub.

10 Soap: yes, soap. What are you looking at me like that for? They still make soap, you know.

CROSSWORD

CLUES

ACROSS:

2 Some men aspire to be one; some women aspire to change their identity just to avoid one. (9)

4 The number of times you've left the house on time with the children. (4)

5 The day you do all your Tuesday chores. (9)

7 You'll be on your hands and knees picking this out of the carpet, long after your daughter's birthday. (7)

8 The place where all your guitars go to rest. (7)

9 You once wrote to Amazon about the sheer amount of this stuff they delivered to you for a small pocket guide to Bali. (9)

10 You promised you wouldn't obsess over it but, well, here it is. (4)

11 You used to obsess over it. Not so much now. (5)

DOWN:

1 The mythical abode of the dead, imagined as being under the earth, OR the name of the roller coaster ride at that relatively inexpensive theme park you take the children to every public holiday. (10)

3 What you display on any sporting fields these days. (10, 4, 2, 7)

6 An acronym most commonly associated with discovering how much *Peppa Pig* toys cost. (3)

TOP DADS

Identify the card most relevant to you from the following pages – see how your skills fare against the rest of your dad friends.

WORKAHOLIC DAD

STRENGTH: 2

INTELLIGENCE: 87

CREATIVITY: 10

COURAGE: 26

STYLE: 9

PLAYTIME DAD

STRENGTH: 23

INTELLIGENCE: 31

CREATIVITY: 85

COURAGE: 98

STYLE: 4

GEEK DAD

STRENGTH:	5
INTELLIGENCE:	80
CREATIVITY:	76
COURAGE:	10
STYLE:	20

SPORTY DAD

STRENGTH:	90
INTELLIGENCE:	65
CREATIVITY:	64
COURAGE:	82
STYLE:	3

SOCIAL DAD

STRENGTH:	9
INTELLIGENCE:	49
CREATIVITY:	40
COURAGE:	16
STYLE:	78

DIY DAD

STRENGTH:	70
INTELLIGENCE:	10
CREATIVITY:	81
COURAGE:	94
STYLE:	2

GADGET DAD

STRENGTH:	8
INTELLIGENCE:	86
CREATIVITY:	73
COURAGE:	10
STYLE:	3

HIPSTER DAD

STRENGTH:	4
INTELLIGENCE:	88
CREATIVITY:	45
COURAGE:	7
STYLE:	97

Grooming TIPS

THE FULL WORKS

Every now and again it's good to have the full works at your local barber – haircut, shave, hot towel, facial. Plus, a lot of the high-end barbers are too disdainful to make small talk, which is almost as refreshing as the facial.

THE RIGHT PRODUCT

Choose the right hair product for you. If you're losing your hair, remember there are sprays and lighter pomades available that claim they can hold onto the hair you've got left. Now this is a lie, but the older you get the more you rely on grooming products to lie to you.

TRIM ALL NOSE AND EAR HAIR

Some men think that removing this hair somehow emasculates them, as if anyone is going to view the tufts exploding from their nostrils and think, "There's the alpha male I need in my life." Get rid.

LOSE YOUR BACK HAIR

There is a special product on the market for just this job that looks a lot like a big razor. In fact, it is a big razor. That's what it is. But it'll be called something like The Back-Thatch 3000 just so they can ramp up the retail price.

TRIM YOUR FINGERNAILS

Toenails too. Yes, toenails and toes and feet in general are horrifying; that's why God put them as far away from us as possible. But it's good to keep them looking like they don't repel you.

EXCUSES
TO GET OUT OF
Household Chores

- **PUTTING LAUNDRY AWAY** – "I'm very sorry. I appear to have thrown myself down the stairs."

- **VACUUMING** – "I can't right now. There's a rugby sevens match just starting."

- **CLEARING THE TABLE** – "But I cleared the table in 2017."

- **WASHING THE DISHES** – "I can't get my smartwatch wet."

- **WALKING THE DOG** – "I sold the dog."

- **MOPPING THE FLOORS** – "I sold all the floors."

- **MAKING DINNER** – "Remember what happened last time I made dinner? No, me neither. That's what smoke inhalation does to you."

- **WASHING THE CAR** – "I can't right now. There's highlights of a rugby sevens third-place play-off match just starting."

- **LOADING THE DISHWASHER** – "I've never loaded a dishwasher correctly in my entire life. Your request is just not in your best interest. Also, I can't get my smartwatch wet."

Holiday CODE-CRACKER

To crack the code, figure out which letter corresponds to which number. Some starter letters have been provided in key, just to get you going!

1 B	2	3	4	5 Y	6	7	8	9	10	11	12 U	13
14	15	16	17	18	19	20	21	22	23	24	25	26

CLUES:

1. A holiday location you regret as soon as you arrive.

   _____

   (1, 9, 22, 13, 19)

2. You will inevitably pay four times more than you intended here for something you never wanted.

   _____

   (1, 22, 3, 22, 22, 2)

3. These British crossings mean drivers will slow down before running you over.

   _____

   (3, 9, 1, 2, 22)

4. A religious building with a gift shop that charges an obscene amount of money for a dish towel.

   _____

   (22, 1, 1, 9, 5)

ANSWERS:

1. BEACH, 2. BAZAAR, 3. ZEBRA, 4. ABBEY

16

CLUES:

5. The space you stare into when you realize you'll be paying an obscene amount of money for a dish towel.

   _____

   (22, 1, 5, 6, 6)

6. What you feel like doing when you hand over an obscene amount of money for a dish towel.

   _____

   (7, 5, 10, 4, 8)

7. What you turn when you walk down the street in your salmon-coloured holiday combat shorts.

   _____

   (19, 9, 22, 7, 6)

8. As a dad on holiday, consider yourself under-____.

   _____

   (6, 9, 11, 9, 7)

9. Nevertheless, you still think about this.

   _____

   (6, 9, 11)

10. You make a point of buying one only to leave it at home on your bedside table.

    _____

    (8, 12, 10, 7, 9)

11. A company that arranges your holiday even though it's not that difficult really.

    _____

    (22, 8, 9, 4, 13, 5)

12. Run these down a chalkboard instead of watching the hotel entertainment.

    _____

    (4, 22, 10, 14, 6)

ANSWERS:

5. ABYSS, 6. DYING, 7. HEADS, 8. SEXED, 9. SEX, 10. GUIDE, 11. AGENCY, 12. NAILS

CLUES:

13. What you feel like after spending an obscene amount of money on a dish towel.

    _____
    (10, 7, 10, 15, 16)

14. You're more likely to see these than a genuine pair of Nike shoes at the local market.

    _____
    (5, 9, 16, 10, 6)

15. Nothing on holiday is this.

    _____
    (9, 22, 6, 5)

16. A 5-minute stroll along the local docks makes you an expert on these.

    _____
    (5, 22, 13, 19, 16, 6)

17. The hotel bar after 10:30 p.m.

    _____
    (7, 2, 5)

18. For blocking out the sound of children on your flight, particularly your own.

    _____
    (9, 22, 2, 1, 12, 7, 6)

19. You will inevitably do this in the bar and your wife will go back to your room.

    _____
    (7, 22, 1)

20. You worked on these before the holiday for about 20 minutes but somehow you don't look like The Rock.

    _____
    (22, 1, 6)

CLUES:

21. You definitely have the best body at the pool.

    _____
    (10, 6, 19)

22. Attentive, kind, helpful... and invisible when you actually need them.

    _____
    (6, 16, 22, 17, 17)

23. The number of staff in your vicinity when you don't need them.

    _____
    (6, 10, 11)

24. Your wife approaches you at the hotel disco and advises you that sometimes it's good to be this.

    _____
    (6, 19, 5)

25. It's your job to stifle these when making conversation with your fellow guests.

    _____
    (5, 22, 18, 4, 6)

26. Your dive into the pool.

    _____
    (22, 1, 20, 9, 13, 16)

27. Don't try to act cool around it, it will only make it much, much worse.

    _____
    (4, 12, 7, 10, 16, 5)

Colouring

SPOT THE DIFFERENCE

THIS DAD HAS OVERDRESSED FOR THE OFFICE PARTY. SPOT THE 10 DIFFERENCES.

Dad Jokes ?

When one door closes another one opens. In summary, this submarine just isn't workable.

I suffer from "Incorrect Acronym Syndrome" or "PBZ".

When weather forecasters say the country is covered in fog patches, does that mean the country is trying to quit fog?

"Do you want to go and see that film with Hugo Weaving in it?" "Sounds a bit boring. Does he do anything else?"

My boss just emailed to say my "latest work is outstanding", which was rather presumptuous of him because I haven't even done it yet.

LoL!

I once worked in a beer factory but the boss had me jumping through hops! Seriously though, I left due to poor safety standards.

Ha, Ha!

I'm blessed because I do what I love every day: disappoint my children.

Thanks to all the police horses for keeping criminal horses off our streets.

My wife accused me today of lacking spontaneity, so I've started a spreadsheet of possible ripostes.

I just signed up to a website and made my password the location of my honeymoon and the site said it was "weak". Well I'm sorry but it was all I could afford at the time.

I've mounted a landline phone next to my bathroom mirror because every now and then I like to pretend I'm visiting my twin in jail.

LOL!

Catwoman should have a nemesis called Curiositywoman.

Why didn't the skeleton go to the party? He has two children.

Fun Fact: to ensure precise landings, aeroplane pilots imagine the runway is a giant baby's mouth.

Where do you go in the office when you want to chat about water coolers?

Goldfish don't do anything and have castles. So, in a way, goldfish are doing better than you.

Ha, Ha!

Robert Downey Jr should continue playing Iron Man because it's his strong suit.

"In the future, everyone will be famous for 15 minutes." – That guy with the hair, I forget his name.

"I have two pets but I'm allergic to them." "That's a paradox." "No, it's a pair of cats."

Dad Dance Moves

A comprehensive guide to the dance moves you need to know as a dad.

THE SIDE TO SIDE
Often used on the dancefloor to guarantee no one looks at you. The stepping may become bouncy once confidence is gained/ alcohol is drunk.

USING YOUR ELBOWS
This can be used with the move above. Imagine you're holding an imaginary tray of drinks in front of you. Now you no longer have weird static arms!

THE TWIST
Possibly the first step toward what we now know as dad dancing. Despite being over 50 years old, this is still very much the dance of choice for dads at wedding discos.

SHUFFLE DANCING
This is an easy one but you have to stay fit to maintain it. Otherwise you'll lose your rhythm and you'll just look like you're running for a bus.

THE MACARENA
The greatest trick this song pulls is making you want to listen to the tune so you can dance to it, despite the fact it's officially the worst song ever made. Very clever.

FLOSSING
This is a good move which demonstrates excellent rhythm and technique. However being a dad you may kill the move stone dead if you do it in public so please be careful.

GANGNAM STYLE
Not the most alluring dance move but a good one if you prefer to let loose. Requires good hand–eye coordination and total lack of self-awareness.

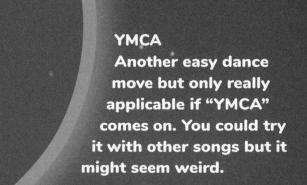

YMCA
Another easy dance move but only really applicable if "YMCA" comes on. You could try it with other songs but it might seem weird.

FACTFILE
#1: BIKES

1 While filming the *Matrix* films, Keanu Reeves bought every stuntman in the crew a £6,000 Harley-Davidson motorcycle, firmly cementing his position as the man for whom your wife would definitely ditch you.

2 Evel Knievel became an instant household name in 1968 because of a crash that was televised on ABC's *Wide World of Sports*. He cleared the fountains at Caesar's Palace but crashed as he landed. It's also worth noting that a renowned physicist died on the same day as Evel Knievel – 30 November 2007 – meaning the newspapers could have gone with the headline "Evel Dead Too". They chose not to.

3 In motorcycle road racing the paramedics ride superbikes in order to keep up with the participants in case of a crash. If the paramedics crash, there is a standby team to assist them. And if the standby team crash then... well, then they're on their own. Otherwise it looks a bit ridiculous.

4 The penny-farthing was invented before the bicycle, proving that in the 1880s, people were more interested in injuring themselves in an entertaining way than actually travelling anywhere.

TOP 10

MEN'S GADGETS

1 Activity tracker: this revolutionary accessory is a must for every health-conscious dad who not only wants to monitor how many steps he does in a day, but also wants to talk about it at great length, ensuring everyone around him soon increases their step quota for the day too.

2 Swiss army knife: a contraption dating back to the late 1890s, this distinctive gadget is still seen as an essential tool by many dads for a variety of daring situations from peeling a potato when the peeler is in the dishwasher to showing off to a child.

3 Video doorbell: if you're out and about but you want to maintain your hobby of spying on frustrated delivery drivers, this is the ideal gadget for you.

4 3D printer: the 3D printer is every dad's dream – providing your dream is to make small ineffectual plastic toys that many would generously call "crude".

5 Segway: if you've ever walked somewhere and thought "there must be a more ludicrous way of doing this", then may we suggest an unsafe podium on wheels?

6 Drone: a perfect gadget for any dad with a passion for aerial photography, general surveillance or crashing objects in fields.

7 Thermostat app: the gadget that turns that inexplicable dad-like devotion to room temperature into a full-blown obsession.

8 PlayStation VR: for the dad who needs to escape to a world of ultra-violence and horror because he can't deal with the pressures of making school lunches and being on bath-time duty.

9 GoPro: for those numerous occasions when your family and friends feel like watching an unedited 30-km bike ride.

10 Spy camera pen: you'll feel like James Bond with one of these – if James Bond had absolutely no spying to do and wanted to risk arrest for voyeurism.

A TO Z OF COOL DADS

ASHTON KUTCHER

Ashton and his wife Mila Kunis do not give presents to their children on Christmas Day because they prefer a modest, traditional Christmas (in their six-bedroom beach house in Santa Barbara… okay, we might be a bit jealous).

BARACK OBAMA

Governing the country and raising a family at the same time, President Obama hoped that both his daughters and the country would flourish under his guidance for years to come. Well, the girls turned out great.

CHRIS HEMSWORTH

Rumour has it that even Chris Hemsworth whipping out his Thor wig can't distract his wife enough to stop her asking him to change his children's diapers. Frankly, if this doesn't work, then nothing will.

DAVID BECKHAM

Not only the father of four children but also the father of the early twenty-first century Mohican which is still sported by British estate agents to this day.

EDDIE MURPHY

If ever you want to feel like you've not achieved enough in life, look no further than Eddie Murphy. Not only is he father to ten children (that's right, ten) but he's also starred in more than five times that number of films. Still, at least you managed to shower today.

FREDDIE PRINZE JR

The Scooby-Doo actor is one of those few Hollywood actors who can actually show his children the bulk of his movie work. As yet, they have asked him not to.

GORDON RAMSAY

Not everyone can be as skilled as Gordon Ramsay in the kitchen, and some dads worry that they won't be able to pass down any culinary skills to their kids. Rest assured, most children would rather eat fish fingers and chips than roasted garlic and lime shrimp alfredo tortellini anyway.

HUGH GRANT

Rumour has it the Bridget Jones star is very protective of his daughter and insists that she keeps her old baby monitor switched on in her bedroom until she's at least 21.

IDRIS ELBA

The top TV actor has said that when he was a new parent, he felt an overwhelming sense of good fortune. If we were up against *The Wire*, we'd say having Idris as a dad means his children are the fortunate ones.

JOHN LEGEND

One of the coolest dads in Hollywood – mainly because his cooler wife tweets cool things and takes cool pictures of their cool children.

KANYE WEST

Sometimes it seems like an injustice that celebrities can call their children names like "Psalm" and "Saint" and they're somehow even more cool. Meanwhile, you call your child "Sunday School" and get nothing but ridicule.

LENNY KRAVITZ

Lenny was so committed to being a cool dad in the beginning that he set up a "Babies' Book Club" where babies could sit around and discuss books they were reading. However, the main topic each time was how crinkly they were and how the little mirror at the end felt "too predictable".

MARK WAHLBERG

Another very cool dad, though reportedly very competitive. Apparently, when a cooing admirer remarked one day that his young baby was "looking so strong", he promptly lifted some heavy furniture above his head through fear of being undermined.

EIL PATRICK HARRIS

Mr Harris is a committed dad, though sometimes he takes his dedication too far. Reportedly, he once he gave a lecture to just his kids entitled "*Peppa Pig*: Why is there a vet and a doctor?".

OSCAR ISAAC

Apparently, the Star Wars star refuses to put his young son in "unrealistic T-shirts" that say things like "brave pirate" or "world's greatest astronaut". "I still need to cut up his food! I love him, but this guy's not ready for NASA."

PAUL WELLER

The Jam frontman named his twin sons John Paul and Bowie after his musical heroes. I did the same with my two boys, Amadeus and Slipknot.

QUENTIN TARANTINO

Qs are notoriously hard in these lists, but luckily Quentin Tarantino has recently become a father – talk about good timing!

RYAN REYNOLDS

Ryan Reynolds loves his children so much he doesn't mind that period when your toddler wakes you up by climbing into your bed and headbutting you.

SERGIO GARCÍA

The accomplished Spanish golfer named his daughter Azalea, after the flowers that Augusta National Golf Club is known for. Just as well they weren't growing any Brazilian Dutchman's Pipes.

TOM HANKS

Imagine this for a second: your father is Woody from *Toy Story*. I mean, how cool is that? Okay he's also technically the dude in all the Dan Brown films but look, life isn't perfect.

USAIN BOLT

Usain Bolt will be a great father one day. You could easily see him doing the unglamorous dad duties like picking up dropped crayons in restaurants. Definitely. Look, U is difficult too okay. Give me a break.

VIN DIESEL

His Fast and Furious franchise may have made him the personification of Hollywood machismo but that doesn't mean Vin Diesel doesn't know how to do a mean packed lunch in the morning or know where his daughter's favourite hairbrush is.

WILL SMITH

Will Smith and his children are so good together. Except in films.

XAVI

Apart from lecturing his daughter regularly that *PAW Patrol* isn't a sensible business model, the former Barcelona soccer star is a very cool dad. (It's true, by the way, when the pups grow up, they won't fit inside their vehicles. I mean, what were they thinking?)

YO-YO MA

The Chinese-American cellist was himself a child prodigy but that doesn't mean he has heaped any enormous expectations onto his two children, Genius and Virtuoso Ma.

ZINEDINE ZIDANE

The Real Madrid manager is so cool, he'd even look calm and collected in a children's soft-play centre. You should see him wading out of a soft-play ball pit; he looks like Daniel Craig as James Bond, emerging from the water.

QUIZ

Which British sporting competition, first held in 1829, had its closest finish in 2003 – a winning margin of 1 ft (30 cm) – and finally became exciting?

The University Boat Race.

Which church is perhaps best known for holding mass weddings for its members (sometimes known as "Moonies"), most of whom haven't known each other long enough to have their first argument?

The Unification Church.

"Lesser great leaf-nosed" and "lesser horseshoe" are what kind of creatures?

Bats. Luckily DC Comics never went into specifics. Otherwise we could have had Lesser Great Leaf-Nosed Batman.

What nationality was Picasso?

Spanish. Unless you've watched the Anthony Hopkins biopic in which case any answer is correct.

Bluto is which cartoon character's enemy?

Popeye.

What do your general knowledge and your lacrimal glands have in common?

They both produce tears.

What does BMW stand for?

Bavarian Motor Works, or Breath-taking Misuse of the Wheel.

On 6 February 1971, where was a golf ball hit for the first time?

The Moon. And an extra point for the follow-up question: was this really the best use of their time?

Which city did Raymond Chandler describe as having the personality of a paper cup?

Los Angeles. Chandler was forced to retract his comments after much criticism from fans of paper cups.

Who was England's first Tudor king?

Henry VII. This is the king you inevitably skip at school to get to Henry VIII who, let's face it, is box office.

SPOT THE DIFFERENCE

THIS DAD HAS TAKEN HIS VICTORY AT "FAMILY GAMES NIGHT" A BIT TOO SERIOUSLY. SPOT THE 10 DIFFERENCES.

Bedtime Stories For Dads

The Keys

It's at around five to nine that they all convene by the school gate. Each one of them holds a bunch of keys: car keys, house keys, miscellaneous keys.

Of course, these bunches of keys are inevitably branded by a particular key-ring accessory, such as a small photo of their children encased in plastic, or something a little more fanciful like a spiky rainbow-coloured rubber ball.

Every parent feels the need to convey their busy lifestyles through their keys. The more keys you have, the busier you are; the busier you are, the more popular you are.

One morning, I decided enough was enough. This symbolic posturing had to be punctured and I was the parent to do it. I had the clique by the school gates in my sights, for despite the fact that I had seven keys on my key-ring they never let me join their huddle. Well, that was all going to end very soon. I was going to make them sit up and take notice of me.

On Tuesday evening I set to work hanging the most elaborate and ornate set of keys on my key-ring for a showdown the next day. The following keys were attached:

- A large copper-coloured key from my garden shed.
- A tiny gold key with a circular head, courtesy of my ex-wife's abandoned jewellery box.
- A key from a Victorian prison that washed up near my ex-best-friend's beach house.
- A swimming-pool locker key encased in a small luminous orange cylinder.
- A unicorn-shaped key that my daughter bought with 150 redemption tickets.
- A selection of ornate keys handed down to me by my father who for 25 years was the general administrator at Windsor Castle.

On Wednesday morning, after I dropped off Amelia-Blue at the main entrance, I walked back toward the school gates and saw them: the huddle. I strode meaningfully toward them holding my cumbersome yet beguiling set of keys. I tried to fold my arms and let the keys hang nonchalantly off my fingers as they nestled underneath my elbow.

Unfortunately, the combined weight of the keys – particularly the castle keys – caused my body to tilt. I decided to hold them by my side and occasionally swing them over my hand – though this too was difficult to execute successfully.

As I passed the revered huddle, I slowed down to observe the fallout. A few of the group had become dazzled by the sight of my spectacular bunch. They knew. They knew I had somewhere to go, something to do, someone to be.

I passed the gaggle confidently, involuntarily jingling and jangling as I went. Not a word was spoken but I knew I had caused a ripple among the parental elite.

No one had seen as many keys as these.

Soon I would be infiltrating this clique, making my moves, assuming my position. Soon I would be calling the shots.

After passing them, I had to stop briefly to pick up the tiny jewellery- box key which had inadvertently flung off the ring and bounced into the road. As I stepped off the kerb to pick it up, I felt the hot mesh grill of an Audi A6 bury itself into my left shoulder.

I hit the tarmac with a crack. My glasses snapped in two and flew into the air independently of each other.

As the driver was an Audi owner, I inevitably received little compassion from him. Luckily the criticism and general name-calling that he directed toward me was muffled by the blood in my ears which I could feel filling up inside me like an espresso machine.

I looked at the huddle one last time. As expected, every single one of them was looking at me. My keys had nearly got me killed but ultimately, they had served their purpose. The hierarchy was going to change.

I picked up both halves of my glasses and limped back to the pavement. I decided to sit on a nearby garden wall momentarily to both collect my wits and assess any significant damage to my body.

The driver returned to his car and shouted "key tosser" before getting back in and driving away.

I concluded that I should wait until the clique had dispersed before I passed out or fell backward off the garden wall.

But at the end of the day, there was no doubt about it. I had made my mark.

HOW TO BE LIKE...

To be a parent you need to have understanding and be protective, but at the same time keep your distance; Billy Ray Cyrus is a perfect example of a dad who has mastered this particular set of skills. Although, if your child wants to swing naked on a wrecking ball, do make sure there's supervision.

BILLY RAY CYRUS

Men think they'll lose their youth and their looks when they have children, but take a look at Chris Pratt, for whom the opposite is true. In fact, it's not clear how he did this. It's one of life's mysteries.

CHRIS PRATT

Sir Paul was famously inspired by his children and wrote songs just for them. So, if you think having children robs you of your creativity, think again. Saying that, you're obviously not going to be as good as Paul McCartney because... well, he's a Beatle. I mean come on, be realistic. But good luck!

SIR PAUL McCARTNEY

Even though his son John has followed in his footsteps to become an actor, Denzel has been careful not to overshadow his son's career. Admittedly, comparing the shade cast by your career to that of Denzel Washington is like comparing the shadow of a sequoia to a pot of parsley – but the moral is in there for you somewhere.

DENZEL WASHINGTON

A lot of dads feel they won't have time for the gym after children, but look at Jason Momoa. Seriously, look at him! Okay, maybe don't look at him any more; you'll start to feel worthless.

JASON MOMOA

Being a dad does not rob you of your style, as Jeff Goldblum aptly demonstrates. Unless you had no style to begin with, in which case keep wearing the red combat shorts and brown loafers.

JEFF GOLDBLUM

Some dads think their brains will be dulled by having a big family, like somehow they won't be alert or sharp any more. Well, take a look at Mick Jagger, who has so many children and grandchildren that you'd forgive him for mistaking his offspring for his offspring's offspring.

SIR MICK JAGGER

Do you fear that being a dad means you'll no longer be one of the boys? Well Prince Harry is seen as being one and not only is he a dad but he also spent most of his life being chauffeured around in a giant gold carriage with his grandmother. If he can maintain his image as one of the boys, so can you.

PRINCE HARRY

If you're worried that becoming a father may mean losing your edge, remember that Dave Grohl is still very much a rock god despite having children. The only concern you should have is that they'll have your edgy gene and become more edgy than you. Which they will. Unfortunately, that's something we can't help you with.

DAVE GROHL

As a father of daughters, you may think that most of the time you're just going to be worrying about every aspect of their lives. And you'd be right. But look at Steven Tyler and his daughters. Does he look like he lets worry get to him? No. And they're otherworldly. Admittedly he's so slight, worry wouldn't be able to locate him in the first place.

STEVEN TYLER

DOs AND DON'Ts OF DAD FASHION

DO

Plain T-shirt

DON'T

T-shirt with band name/graphics. You're a dad; you don't have to pretend to like cool bands and brands any more.

DO

Combat shorts

DON'T

Combat shorts with anything in the pockets

DO

Baseball cap

DON'T

Baseball cap back to front if you're 35 or over

DON'T

Vest on its own. You're not Bruce Willis. Not even Bruce Willis is Bruce Willis these days.

DO

Vest with shirt

DO

Smart shirt

DON'T

Smart shirt open with T-shirt underneath. This somehow makes two nice garments look bad.

DON'T

Baggy jeans that look like you started putting them on but then forgot to see it through. And skinny jeans. "Skinny" is an adjective you shouldn't bother yourself with any more.

DO

Jeans that fit

DO

Dark red chinos

DON'T

Salmon pink jeans. Unless you've got a clashing jumper to tie over your shoulders to complete the "arrogant tourist" look.

DO

Stylish watch

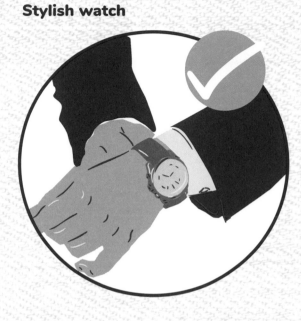

DON'T

Leather/beaded bracelets. You have a mortgage and two cars; you're not selling drugs at a music festival.

DO

Straw trilby

DON'T

Bucket hat. It's called a bucket hat for goodness' sake. Of course it won't look good on you.

A GREAT DAD IS...

1 Always a great storyteller at bedtime, even though he's read *Peppa Pig and the Fire Engine* 67,987 times.

2 Able to re-enact Star Wars, *The Lego Movie*, etc. first thing in the morning before his first coffee of the day.

3 Willing to make an entire costume that ties in with the theme of his child's school's literature week from scratch. And because his child didn't tell him about it, he has an hour to make it before school. And the theme this year is the work of F. Scott Fitzgerald.

4 Totally cool with it every time his child's drinks bottle breaks. Which it will do. Hourly. Because our society has somehow forgotten how to make drinks bottles without them being fragile receptacles that break if filled with liquid or used for drinking.

5 Always prepared to adjust to all the new rules his child imposes for any game they wish to play so that they win every time. Even if it's Snap.

6 Happy in the knowledge that he won't consume his toast when it pops out of the toaster nor sip his coffee the moment it's poured. Those days are over.

7 Not concerned that he knows every line from *Thomas and the Magic Railroad* but forgets occasionally what he does for a living.

8 At peace with the fact that you have a few kids' apps on your phone and so therefore you'll never have a clean screen again.

9 Always aware that if his children go to bed 2 hours late, they'll wake up the next morning precisely 2 seconds later than normal.

10 An expert in telling his child to put their shoes on around fifty times a day without losing his mind.

FACTFILE

#2: TOOLS

1 A selection of tools unearthed in Kenya in 1969 were discovered to be over 3 million years old. Further research has revealed that they had been borrowed by a man who promised to return them to his neighbour later that afternoon.

2 To this day, every Swiss military recruit receives a Swiss army knife upon beginning their service. No one knows if recent financial cutbacks will alter this tradition, although they have ordered more Christmas crackers this year.

3 In 1914 S. Duncan Black and his friend Alonzo Decker modified the cumbersome C. & E. Fein power drill by giving it a pistol grip similar to a Colt .45. This is the electric drill from which all electric drills descended. The pistol grip also meant one person could drill on their own without needing help, thereby giving birth to the "leave me alone. I know what I'm doing" attitude adopted by dads on all public holidays.

4 Most scissors are made to work best for people who are right-handed. This is because the inventor of the scissors was left-handed and he wanted to burden right-handed people with doing all cutting-related work forever.

Dad JOKES ?

What's white and can't climb trees?
A fridge.

Do you want to hear a word I just made up? Plagiarism.

If you ever get cold, just stand in the corner for a bit. They are usually around 90 degrees.

A woman told me she recognized me from the vegetarian club, but I'd never met herbivore.

A friend of mine died recently after drinking a gallon of varnish. It was a horrible end, but a lovely finish.

LOL!

I wouldn't buy anything with Velcro. It's a total rip-off.

Ha, Ha!

RIP boiled water. You will be mist.

I'm not addicted to brake fluid. I can stop whenever I want.

What do you call a man with no nose and no body? Nobody nose.

TOP
OF THE HOPS

RANK THE FOLLOWING BEER STYLES FROM ONE TO TEN, IN ORDER OF PREFERENCE.

Pilsner

$\frac{}{10}$

Lambic

$\frac{}{10}$

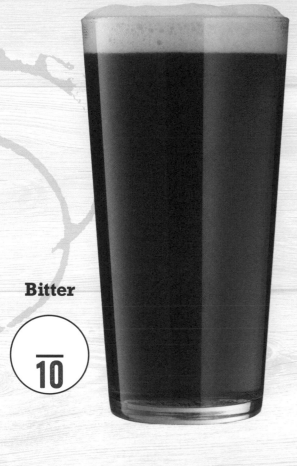

Bitter

$\overline{10}$

India pale ale (IPA)

$\overline{10}$

Porter

$\overline{10}$

Dry stout

$\overline{10}$

Barley wine

$\overline{10}$

Imperial
stout

$\overline{10}$

Golden
ale

$\overline{10}$

Pale ale

$\overline{10}$

DAD RECIPES

Cheese sandwich

Method:

★ First take the two slices of bread and put them side by side on a chopping board. Hopefully, the bread will already be sliced, but if you've accidentally bought a fresh unsliced loaf, then you'll need to get a bread knife and slice it yourself like you're making a sandwich in the days of yore or something.

★ Butter the slices of bread, or if you have margarine, margarine the slices of bread. Make sure to cover every area of the bread.

★ Take the one or more slices of cheese and place it on one slice of bread.

★ Then take the other slice of bread (the slice that has no cheese on it) and put it on top of the slice of bread that does have cheese on it. Preferably, place it butter-side down.

★ This is basically your cheese sandwich. You are quite welcome to cut it down the middle or diagonally if you're cultured but personally, I like to bite into the whole thing. Oh, and if you're in company, remember to use a plate.

You will need:

★ **Two slices of bread**
★ **A slice of cheese (maybe two)**
★ **Butter or margarine**

Tomato soup

Method:

★ First take the tin of soup and open it with a tin opener. Pour the soup into a saucepan and turn up the heat on the stove. You can stir the soup with a wooden spoon if you wish.

★ Once you feel the soup is heated through sufficiently, pour it into a bowl. There are bowls available that are specifically designed for soup, but I've found any bowl is good enough.

★ You may want a piece of bread to go with it because soup is unremittingly dull.

You will need:

★ **A tin of tomato soup**

Beans on toast

Method:

★ First take the two slices of bread and put them in a toaster – one slot each.

★ While your bread is toasting, open the tin of beans with a tin opener and pour them into a saucepan.

★ Heat the beans and stir occasionally with a wooden spoon. Alternatively, you could microwave them in a microwaveable tub – but it would take some of the "cooking" element out of this recipe. You want to feel you've achieved something after all.

★ Once your bread has toasted, butter one side of each slice. Pour the beans out of the saucepan or tub directly on to the toast.

★ Voila! Beans on toast. That's virtually a meal, so you should be proud of yourself.

You will need:

★ **A tin of beans**
★ **Two slices of bread**
★ **Butter or margarine**

WORD SEARCH

CENTRAL HEATING

A lot of dads are obsessed with the temperature of their home so here's a special word search just for those dads who can't leave the radiators alone.

```
O R J H C N R Y L R R T U D G Q A E A F
F J K G L R T V E T H E S D H F M S D E
F W B U N U C T H J T M T L I K M L I M
U W J Q U A A E W M K P V A Q X G L T B
S I I R U W R M A K R E Z E W H B R S Z
I I A P T M B S F E C R I L M D K A U Q
O Z C O O S M D D H E A T I N G L D W S
Q G H S A F X L U Q Q T B Q J V T O L P
S Q T U W V N O K I T U U O Z Z Y G C I
Y A N O D Y D G N T T R C G I Z F J W P
T A G Q Z S V O J J O E T K K L Z B G E
S K V E K I L L Q Y H X F X Q S E N G S
L A I D T S U J D A S Z P H Y C X R U G
Z A G N M A V K G Q T P R Y K C W S I V
J D I H W C I B U B I K B F Q I L X J D
H R P G U X X N S L D O R X T G H J Y E
I F R E R F X L M G O T D U K E L Q A F
V C B C P W S D P Y G M B H N C T A E Y
X K K X F J J Z P V Q P V E P X L T V O
R P U L Y L U X E A G D Z O B T L O G U
```

COLD WATER
THERMOSTAT
HEATING
HOT WATER
BOILER
ADJUST DIAL
PIPES
TEMPERATURE
SAUNA
GOD IT'S HOT

Riddles

1

* I'm taller than you but smaller than you.

* You fear me despite my diminutive appearance.

* Sometimes I'm not even there and you're still petrified of me.

* I take photographs for a living though my prices are very steep.

* I love a game of hide-and-seek. Though by the time you've found me, I've already won.

2

* You can't wake up without smelling what I produce.

* I make a grinding noise in the kitchen about half a dozen times a day.

* I look so futuristic these days I'd be better suited on the Starship *Enterprise* than between your dying spider plant and the bread bin.

* Sometimes you go out and pay an extortionate amount for the same thing I make you every morning. at home. This confuses me.

3

* You can find me on land, sea or rail but I don't take passengers.

* You might find me on a film set but I'm no film star.

* You will often see me on a building site or in a games arcade.

* I can help build a skyscraper or I could win you a cuddly toy.

* Actually I'm rigged a lot of the time so forget the cuddly toy.

ANSWERS:

Brain-Teasers

Q: What breaks every day but no one fixes it?

A: The news.

Q: Which keys don't unlock any door?

A: Piano keys.

Q: Which buds never flower?

A: Earbuds.

Q: Which piano never plays a tune?

A: Your piano.

Q: Why doesn't your piano play a tune?

A: You can't unlock the piano lid.

Q: Why can't you unlock your piano lid?

A: You don't have the piano keys.

Q: What has wings but doesn't fly?

A: The White House.

Q: Where are the piano keys?

A: Under the piano lid, you idiot.

DOT-TO-DOT

Connect the dots to uncover why dad's burgers were so overcooked.

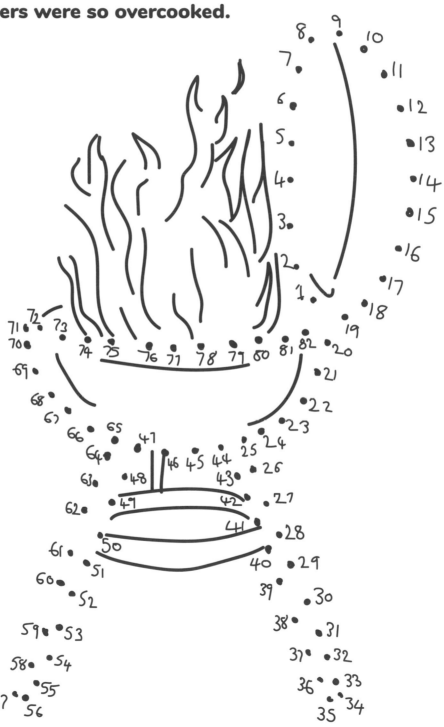

MAZE

Get dad to the bar
before anyone realizes that
he's eaten all his children's
Christmas chocolate.

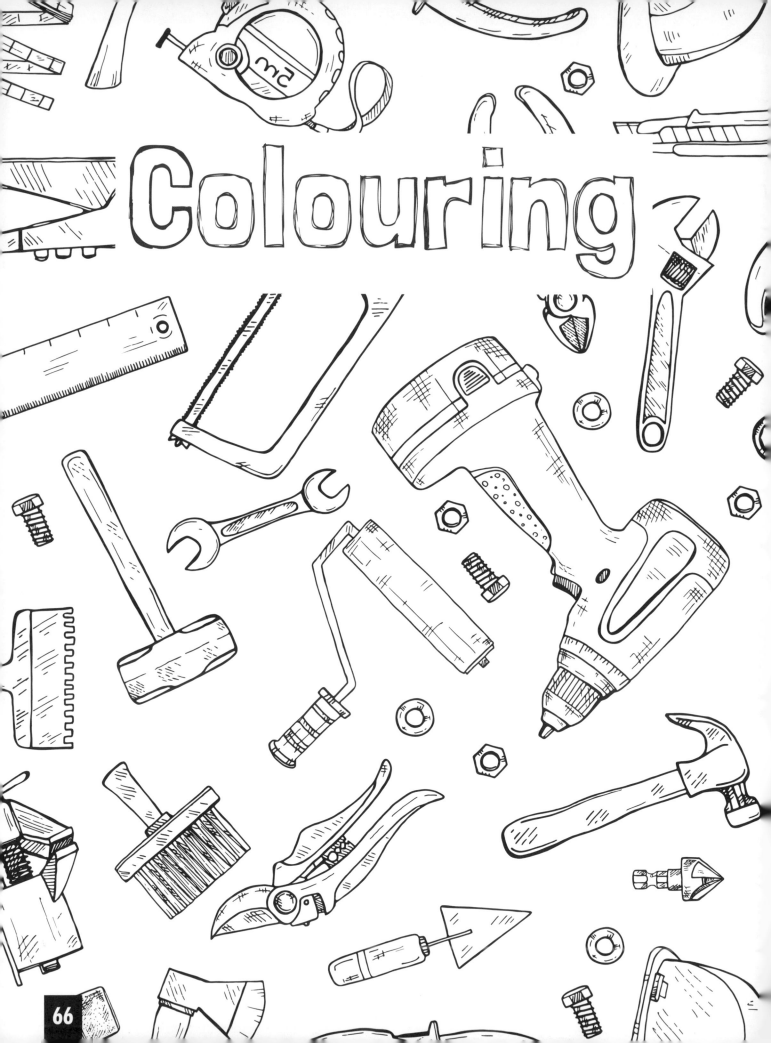

Colouring

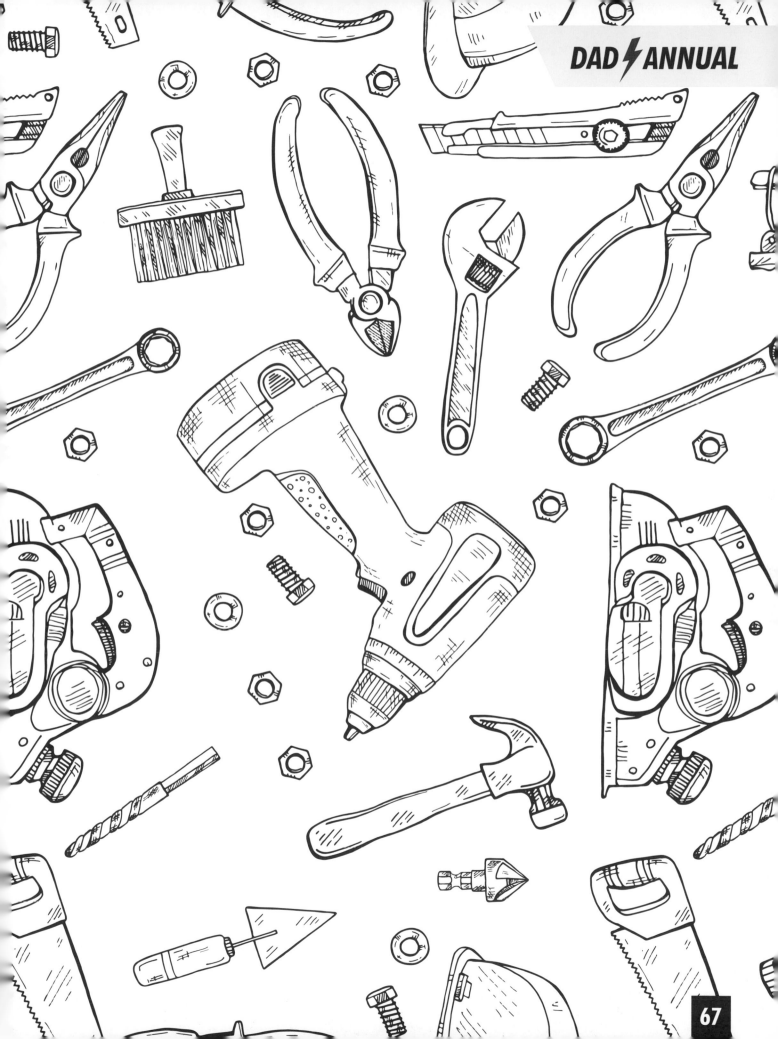

How to Draw

Practise your drawing skills by copying and embellishing this image of a dad at the precise moment he accidentally cuts through the cord with his lawn mower.

Bedtime Stories For Dads

Dad-Discover

We exchanged a few messages on Dad-Discover at first, then we started texting, and before long, we both agreed to meet in a bar not far from where I work.

I felt that since having children I had somehow lost the ability to socialize – to just have a group of friends away from the family dynamic. That's why I joined Dad-Discover, a website dedicated to creating platonic male friendships between disenfranchised fathers.

Now, of course I'd heard about people pretending to be other people online, but I never thought for a moment that I would ever be caught out like that. I think of myself as a pretty shrewd guy, but I hold my hands up: the "dad" I met was not the dad I'd been talking to.

At around 7 p.m. on the night we agreed to meet, several hundred people entered the bar, followed by several hundred more people, until there were around 1,500 people in the bar altogether. I think there were more outside, but they simply couldn't get in.

One of them stepped forward and said to me: "Are you Sean?" I said I was and asked: "Which one of you is Pete?" He then said, "I'm sorry, Sean, there is no Pete. My name is Thomas Dioyogo and I'm the president of Meinhu, a small island country in Micronesia." He then proceeded to sit down and tell me that I had been chosen to succeed him in office. The online profile of Pete was merely a screening process to see if I was suited to take on his job. Every resident of Meinhu was there that night to see if I would accept.

I told President Dioyogo that I was on Dad-Discover looking for companionship. I wasn't looking to govern an island in the western Pacific Ocean. He seemed very disappointed, as did the other 1,500 (or more) inhabitants of Meinhu.

However, the way I look at it is that pretending to be a car mechanic from North London to select someone for a job of that magnitude is – quite frankly – undemocratic.

FACTFILE
#3: BARBECUES

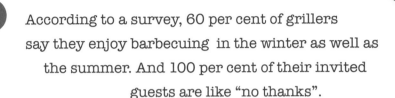

1 According to a survey, 60 per cent of grillers say they enjoy barbecuing in the winter as well as the summer. And 100 per cent of their invited guests are like "no thanks".

2 In 2009, researchers in the Czech Republic found a 4 ft (122 cm) wide roasting pit dating back to 29,000 BC, which contained mammoth ribs and stone tools. This is the earliest recorded example of an outdoor barbecue. Research has also shown that Bill from two doors down came back for a third helping when he thought no one was looking.

3 In an attempt to seal his relationship with Taylor Swift, Calvin Harris allegedly threw her a "vegan-friendly barbecue" – and it worked! Well, for like two weeks or something. Let's not be jealous of Calvin Harris's fame, fortune and assorted beautiful girlfriends; we're just stating a fact here. Let's move on.

4 On the day Prince William and Kate Middleton were married, 7.5 million barbecues took place in the UK. It is believed even Prince Philip whipped up a quick disposable grill on the balcony of Buckingham Palace and cooked half a dozen burgers, with the Queen in charge of salads.

TOP 10

CRAZY LAWS

1 In Switzerland, flushing the toilet after 10 p.m. is considered noise pollution and is banned. But isn't every time technically after 10 p.m.?

2 Chewing gum is banned in Singapore. So, if it's fresh breath you want, keep a toothbrush with you. Oh, and toothpaste. And some sort of portable sink.

3 One of Scotland's old laws states that if a stranger knocks on your door to use the toilet, you must invite them in – unless they're Swiss and it's after 10 p.m. in which case they can take a hike.

4 In San Francisco, it is illegal to feed pigeons because of the sheer amount of excrement they produce. Sadly, there are currently no plans to instate the same legislation against YouTubers in the city.

5 Keeping a fish on its own in Rome is banned, as it is considered to be animal cruelty. Well, the fish don't want to be alone with their thoughts, do they?

6 It is against the law to pee in the ocean in Portugal. Quite how you monitor this is unclear.

7 If you own poultry in Georgia, you must not let them leave your grounds or, in other words, cross the road. Unfortunately, the Georgian joke, "Why did the chicken cross the road?" "It didn't, there are laws," just doesn't scan very well.

8 Swimming pools in France insist men wear Speedos rather than trunks for reasons of hygiene. So, if you see a man wearing trunks in France, you are permitted to walk up to them and say: "I demand you be more uncomfortable."

9 Until recently in Florida, it was illegal for a married woman to go skydiving on a Sunday. But presumably it's still legal to get very drunk and pass mad laws.

10 In Washington State, it is illegal to kill Bigfoot. In case you were looking for some ideas for what to do this weekend.

Horoscopes

Aries

Today you will spend half the day wondering why some supermarkets put plums in containers but put mandarins in nets. Later you will buy a pair of tickets to the Tigers vs Sharks game. You will look forward to this until you realize it's not literal.

Gemini

Someone in your office will use the water you just boiled to make their coffee. Do what you can to resist making a scene. Instead, just plot their downfall over the next 18 months or so.

Leo

You know those panicky seconds when you're pushing your mouse around in circles, trying to find your cursor on the screen? That's how you're going to feel all the time for the rest of the year.

Taurus

You know that idea for a feature film you scribbled down this week? Well, keep hold of that piece of paper because in years to come you can look at it and remember what a good idea it was not to do anything with it because your idea was garbage.

Cancer

Today your bus will stop at a bus stop, open its doors and no one will get on. It will remind you of when you tried online dating.

Virgo

There will be a new Taylor Swift video released this week full of all-star cameos. You won't recognize a single person. This will concern you because you'll think you're somehow irrelevant to modern pop culture. Which you are. Massively.

Libra

Today you will be hot-desking at work. You'll think this makes you sound like a dynamic employee but in reality, it's just an overtly sexy term for people who aren't worthy of basic office furniture.

Sagittarius

Your school teachers said you'd never amount to anything. But, to be fair to them, they didn't know you'd go viral with a video you took of your dog falling into a pond, did they?

Aquarius

You will have a cat problem in your garden this week. An easy way to get rid of unwanted feline intruders is to hang CDs on your trees! Your apparent refusal to modernize musically will confuse them.

Scorpio

You're a trendsetter and this week is no exception. Today you will start pronouncing "encourage" the same as "entourage" hoping others will follow suit. They will not and everyone will look at you strangely. But well done for trying.

Capricorn

This week you will give your phone to a friend to view a picture and they will freely scroll through your photos without asking. They will then find that picture you took of yourself wearing double denim. You will never speak to your friend again.

Pisces

Add some spice into your life by introducing new things in the bedroom! That's right: build a spice rack. A spice rack is very handy if you eat a lot in bed and don't meet people.

ANSWERS

PAGES 8–9 CROSSWORD

UNDERWORLD

WOMANIZER

ASTOUNDINGLACKOFABILIT

ONCE

WEDNESDAY

WTF

GLITTER

STORAGE

PACKAGING

LAWN

STYLE

PAGES 22–23 SPOT THE DIFFERENCE

PAGES 38–39 SPOT THE DIFFERENCE

PAGE 60 WORD SEARCH

```
O R J H C N R Y L R R T U D G Q A E A F
F J K G L R T V E T H E S D H F M S D E
F W B U N U C T H J T M T L I K M L I M
U W J Q U A A E W M K P V A Q X G L T B
S I I R U W R M A K R E Z E W H B R S Z
I I A P T M B S F E C R I L M D K A U Q
O Z C O O S M D D H E A T I N G L D W S
Q G H S A F X L U Q Q T B Q J V T O L P
S Q T U W V N O K I T U U O Z Z Y G C I
Y A N O D Y D G N T R C G I Z F J W P
T A G Q Z S V O J J O E T K L Z B G E
S K V E K I L L Q Y H X F X Q S E N G S
L A I D T S U J D A S Z P H Y C X R U G
Z A G N M A V K G Q T P R Y K C W S I V
J D I H W C I B U B I K B F Q I L X J D
H R P G U X X N S L D O R X T G H J Y E
I F R E R F X L M G O T D U K E L Q A F
V C B C P W S D P Y G M B H N C T A E Y
X K K X F J J Z P V Q P V E P X L T V O
R P U L Y L U X E A G D Z O B T L O G U
```

PAGE 64 MAZE

Image credits

If you're interested in finding out more
about our books, find us on Facebook
at Summersdale Publishers and follow
us on Twitter at @Summersdale.

www.summersdale.com

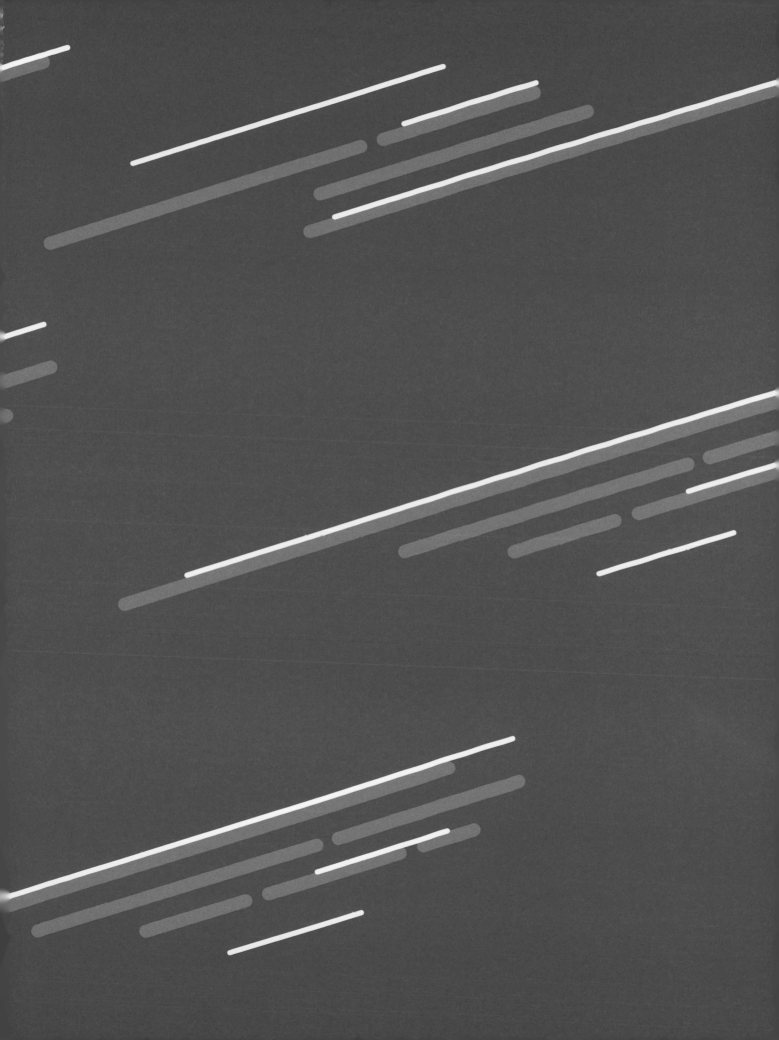

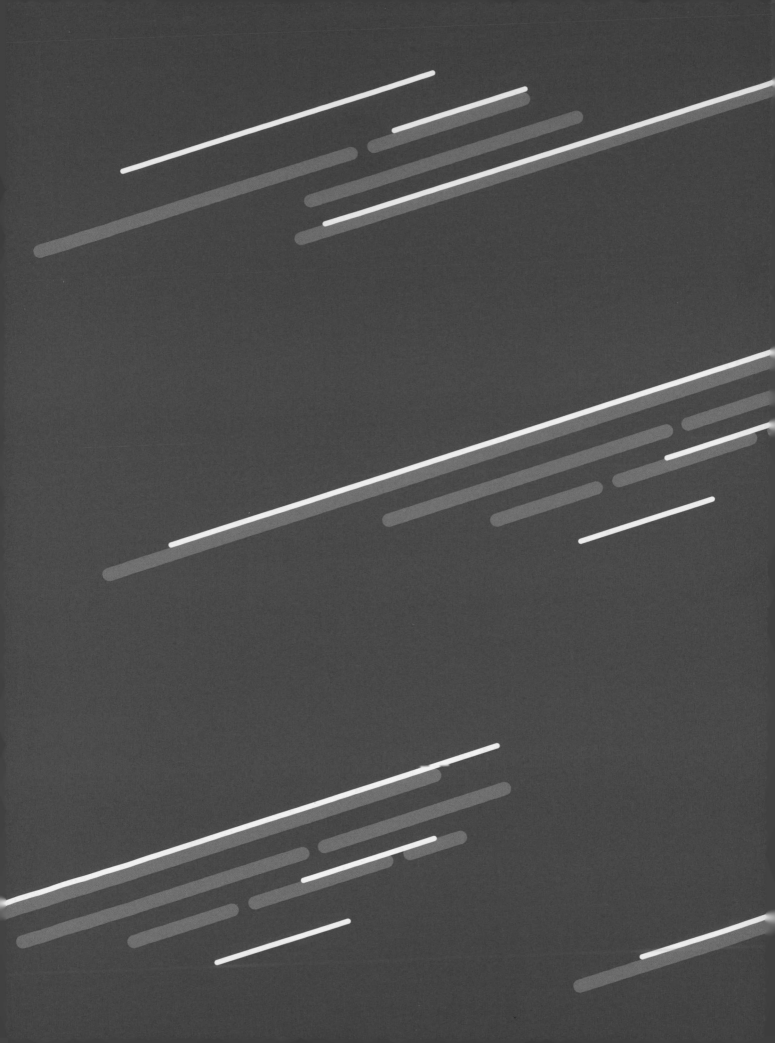